¡Ven conmigo!®

Adelante

Holt Spanish Level 1A

Activities for Communication

HOLT, RINEHART AND WINSTON

Harcourt Brace & Company

Austin • New York • Orlando • Atlanta • San Francisco • Boston • Dallas • Toronto • London

Contributing Writers:

Rosann Batteiger

Mary Diehl

Felicia Kongable

Carol Ann Marshall

Amy Propps

PHOTO/ART CREDITS
Abbreviations used: (c) center, (l) left, (r) right, (bkgd) background.

Photo Credits
All pre-Columbian symbols by EclectiCollections/HRW.
Front cover: (bkgd), © Robert Fried; (c), Joe Viesti/Viesti Associates, Inc.;
Page 38, *Ragazza* Magazine; 49 (tr), Sam Dudgeon/HRW Photo; 49 (bl), NASA/HRW Photo; 50 (all), Marty Granger/Edge
Video Productions/HRW; 53 (tl), Michelle Bridwell/HRW Photo; 55 (all), Mary Glasgow Publications; 59 (cl), Ken Lax/HRW
Photo; 60 (cl), J. M. Childers, USGS/HRW Photo; 63, Sam Dudgeon/HRW Photo; 64 (tr), David Madison/Duomo; 64 (bl),
Focus on Sports.

Art Credits
All work, unless otherwise noted, contributed by Holt, Rinehart & Winston.
Page 1, Edson Campos; 2, Edson Campos; 3, Edson Campos; 4, Edson Campos; 11, Boston Graphics;
12, Boston Graphics; 21, Edson Campos; 22, Edson Campos; 27, Edson Campos; 28, Edson Campos.

Printed in the United States of America

ISBN 0-03-052277-3

1 2 3 4 5 6   021   02 01 00 99 98

Contents

To the Teacher

Oral communication is the most challenging language skill to develop and test. **Adelante** Communicative Activities and Situation Cards help students develop their speaking skills and give them opportunities to communicate in a variety of situations. These information-gap activities, role-plays, and interviews help students make the transition from closed-ended practice to more creative, open-ended use of the language. **Adelante** Realia reproduces authentic documents to provide your students with additional reading and language practice using material written by and for native speakers. Included with the realia are teaching suggestions and student activities. With their focus on dialogue and real-life context, the activities in this book will help your students achieve the goal of interacting with others in Spanish.

Each chapter of *Activities for Communication* provides the following types of communicative practice:

Communicative Activities

In each chapter there are three communicative, pair-work activities that encourage students to express themselves in Spanish in settings where they must seek and share information. The activities provide language practice and also foster cooperative learning. Pair work allows the student to take risks with the language in a relaxed, non-inhibiting, and enjoyable setting. Each communicative activity reflects the content and grammar of the corresponding **paso** in the textbook.

Realia

In each chapter there are three reproducible pieces of realia related to the chapter theme. This collection of material reflects life and culture in Spanish-speaking countries. Finding that they can read and understand documents intended for native speakers, students experience a feeling of accomplishment that encourages them to continue learning. Together with the copying masters of the realia, you will find suggestions for using each document in the classroom to develop listening, speaking, reading, and writing skills.

Situation Cards

For each **paso** of the chapter, three sets of interview questions and three role-plays are provided as copying masters. These cards are designed to stimulate conversation in the classroom. To avoid having to copy the cards repeatedly, consider mounting them on cardboard and laminating them.

Communicative Activities

Communicative Activity 1-1A

1. **Situation** While you're at the mall on Saturday, you run into the new foreign exchange students from your school. Although you haven't met them yet, you recognize them from their school photos.

Task Use the clocks to determine the time of day and greet each of these people appropriately. Ask his or her name, and then ask each person how it's going or how he or she is. Write the information your partner gives you.

MODELO   A — **Buenos días. ¿Cómo te llamas?**
           B — **Me llamo Beatriz.**
           A — **Mucho gusto. ¿Cómo estás?**
           B — **Estoy más o menos.**

| Beatriz | _____ | _____ |
| más o menos | _____ | _____ |

2. Now, pretend to be each of these students and answer your partner's questions.

| Karla | Gonzalo | Julia |
| _____ | _____ | _____ |

How many students are in a good mood? _____ How many are in a bad mood? _____

Communicative Activity 1-1B

COMMUNICATIVE ACTIVITIES

1. Situation While you're at the mall on Saturday, you run into the new foreign exchange students from your school. Although you haven't met them yet, you recognize them from their school photos.

Task Answer your partner's questions, pretending to be each of these students.

MODELO A — Buenos días. ¿Cómo te llamas?
B — Me llamo Beatriz.
A — Mucho gusto. ¿Cómo estás?
B — Estoy más o menos.

Beatriz	Ruperto	Conchita
más o menos		

2. Now switch roles. Use the clocks to determine the time of day and greet each of these students appropriately. Then ask each one's name, how it's going, or how she or he is. Write the information your partner gives you.

Karla	Gonzalo	Julia
triste		

How many students are in a good mood? _____ How many are in a bad mood? _____

Communicative Activity 1-2A

Situation   You're helping your partner sort through the descriptions of pen pals for your Spanish Club. The photos got mislabeled.

Task   Match the descriptions to the photos. Ask your partner for the information you need for numbers two, three, and four. Then answer your partner's questions for numbers five, six, and seven.

MODELO   A — **El número 1, ¿cómo se llama?**
B — **Se llama Juan Antonio Botero.**
A — **¿Cuántos años tiene?**
B — **Tiene 16 años.**
A — **¿Y de dónde es?**
B — **Es de Colombia.**

1.

2.

_____

_____

_____

3.

_____

_____

_____

4.

_____

_____

_____

5.

Pedro Serrano Marín
12 años
España

6.

Pilar Ríos Cabrillo
14 años
Colombia

7.

María Ángeles Castro Barrios
13 años
España

How many of the pen pals are 13 years old? _____ How many are from Spain? _____

Communicative Activity 1-2B

Situation   You're helping your partner sort through the descriptions of pen pals for your Spanish Club. The photos got mislabeled.

Task   Match the descriptions to the photos. Answer your partner's questions for numbers two, three, and four. Then ask your partner for the information you need for numbers five, six, and seven.

MODELO   A — **El número 1, ¿cómo se llama?**
B — **Se llama Juan Antonio Botero.**
A — **¿Cuántos años tiene?**
B — **Tiene 16 años.**
A — **¿Y de dónde es?**
B — **Es de Colombia.**

1.

2.

María Elena Sánchez Orozco
14 años
México

3.

Juan Luis Portillo Benítez
13 años
Guatemala

4.

Lorenzo Malo Hernández
15 años
Ecuador

5.

6.

7.

_____   _____   _____

_____   _____   _____

_____   _____   _____

How many of the pen pals are 13 years old? _____ How many are from Spain? _____

COMMUNICATIVE ACTIVITIES

Nombre _____ Clase _____ Fecha _____

1. **Situation** You and your partner have won a trip to a beach resort for yourselves and your families. The only condition for your prize is that you must both decide on food, music, and recreation. Use the charts below to help you decide.

Task Write down what you like in the second chart. Be sure to have two items for each category. Then ask your partner questions about what he or she wrote and complete the chart below to help you come to an agreement.

MODELO A — ¿Qué deporte te gusta?
　　　　　B — Me gusta el baloncesto.

TU COMPAÑERO/A

	SÍ	NO
Deportes	baloncesto	
Comida		
Música		

2. Now switch roles and answer your partner's questions about what you wrote.

TÚ

	SÍ	NO
Deportes		
Comida		
Música		

Now look at your two completed charts. Do you and your partner have some likes and dislikes

in common? Is there a sport you both like? _____ Is there a food you

both like? _____ What about music? _____

Communicative Activity 1-3B

1. **Situation** You and your partner have won a trip to a beach resort for yourselves and your families. The only condition for your prize is that you must both decide on food, music, and recreation. Use the charts below to help you decide.

Task Write down what you like in the first chart. Be sure to have two items for each category. Then answer your partner's questions about what you wrote.

MODELO A — ¿Qué deporte te gusta?
B — Me gusta el baloncesto.

TÚ

	SÍ	NO
Deportes	baloncesto	
Comida		
Música		

2. Now switch roles and ask your partners questions about what he or she wrote. Complete the chart below.

TU COMPAÑERO/A

	SÍ	NO
Deportes		
Comida		
Música		

Now look at your two completed charts. Do you and your partner have some likes and dislikes

in common? Is there a sport you both like? _____ Is there a food you

both like? _____ What about music? _____

Communicative Activity 2-1A

1. Situation You are a clerk in a bookstore and your partner is a customer.

Task Find out what the customer wants and write his or her order on the receipt below. The bookstore is overstocked on backpacks and erasers, so if your customer doesn't ask for these items, be sure to ask if he or she needs them.

MODELO A — **Buenos días.**
B — **Necesito una mochila y siete cuadernos.**
A — **Muy bien. ¿También necesita unas gomas de borrar?**
B — **No, ya tengo gomas de borrar.**
A — **¿Algo más?**
B — **Sí, necesito...**

Librería Norte
R E C I B O

2. Now switch roles. This time you're the customer and your partner is the clerk. Use your shopping list to tell the clerk what you need.

MODELO B — **Buenas tardes.**
A — **Necesito una mochila y dos carpetas.**
B — **Muy bien. ¿También necesita unos lápices?**
A — **No, ya tengo lápices.**
B — **¿Algo más?**
A — **Sí, necesito...**

Ya tengo...	Necesito...
1 cuaderno	4 cuadernos más
muchas gomas de borrar	3 bolígrafos
1 calculadora	2 carpetas
1 regla	8 lápices
	1 mochila
	1 diccionario

Who bought more items, you or your partner? _____

Communicative Activity 2-1 B

1. **Situation**   You are a customer in a bookstore and your partner is a clerk.

Task   Use your shopping list to tell the store clerk what you need.

MODELO   A — **Buenos días.**
B — **Necesito una mochila y siete cuadernos.**
A — **Muy bien. ¿También necesita unas gomas de borrar?**
B — **No, ya tengo gomas de borrar.**
A — **¿Algo más?**
B — **Sí, necesito..**

Ya tengo...	Necesito...
1 bolígrafo	1 carpeta
2 gomas de	11 lápices
borrar	7 cuadernos
1 diccionario	3 bolígrafos más
	1 mochila
	1 papel

2. Now switch roles. This time you're the clerk and your partner is a customer. The bookstore is overstocked on calculators and pencils, so if your customer doesn't ask for these items, be sure to ask if he or she needs them.

MODELO   B — **Buenas tardes.**
A — **Necesito una mochila y dos carpetas.**
B — **Muy bien. ¿También necesita unos lápices?**
A — **No, ya tengo lápices.**
B — **¿Algo más?**
A — **Sí, necesito...**

Librería Norte

RECIBO

Who bought more items, you or your partner? _____

¡Ven conmigo! Adelante Level 1A, Chapter 2

COMMUNICATIVE ACTIVITIES

Communicative Activity 2-2A

1. **Situation** You and your partner are working at a moving business during the summer. You're supposed to deliver the Rodríguez family's furniture, but you accidentally got the information for the Morales family.

Task Before you arrive at the Rodríguez home, find out from your partner what belongs in each person's room.

MODELO A — ¿Qué necesito poner en el cuarto de Marcos?

B — En el cuarto de Marcos necesitas poner...

CLIENTE: Familia Rodríguez	
NOMBRE	PERTENENCIAS
Marcos	
José	
Carmen	

2. Now answer your partner's questions about the Morales home.

MODELO B — ¿Qué necesito poner en el cuarto de Luisa?

A — En el cuarto de Luisa necesitas poner...

CLIENTE: Familia Morales	
NOMBRE	PERTENENCIAS
Luisa	2 camas, 1 silla, 1 escritorio, 2 lámparas, 1 radio, muchos carteles
Juan	1 cama, 1 escritorio, 1 lámpara, 1 televisor, 2 sillas, 1 reloj
Marta	1 cama, 1 silla, 2 mesas

Who had to move more furniture, you or your partner? _____

Communicative Activity 2-2B

1. **Situation**   You and your partner are working at a moving business during the summer. You're supposed to deliver the Morales family's furniture, but you accidentally got the information for the Rodríguez family.

Task   Answer your partner's questions about the Rodríguez home.

MODELO   A — ¿Qué necesito poner en el cuarto de Marcos?
B — En el cuarto de Marcos necesitas poner...

CLIENTE: Familia Rodríguez	
NOMBRE	**PERTENENCIAS**
Marcos	1 cama, 3 sillas, 1 mesa, unos carteles, 1 radio
José	2 camas, 1 silla, unos carteles, 3 mesas, 1 lámpara
Carmen	1 cama, 2 sillas, 1 televisor, 1 escritorio, 3 lámparas, 1 reloj

2. Before you arrive at the Morales home, find out from your partner what belongs in each person's room.

MODELO   B — ¿Qué necesito poner en el cuarto de Luisa?
A — En el cuarto de Luisa necesitas poner...

CLIENTE: Familia Morales	
NOMBRE	**PERTENENCIAS**
Luisa	
Juan	
Marta	

Who had to move more furniture, you or your partner? _____

1. Situation You have a list of things you need to do this weekend and your partner has a list of things he or she wants to do.

Task Find out if there are things you might be able to do together by telling your partner what you're doing or where you're going. Then ask him or her what he or she wants or needs to do. Write that down next to your list.

MODELO **A — Necesito ir al centro comercial. ¿Qué quieres hacer?**
    B — Quiero comprar ropa.

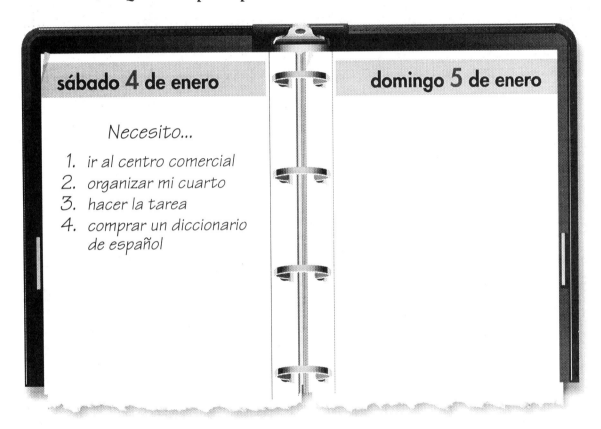

sábado 4 de enero

Necesito...

1. ir al centro comercial
2. organizar mi cuarto
3. hacer la tarea
4. comprar un diccionario de español

domingo 5 de enero

2. Now compare your lists. What will you be able to do together? What won't you be able to do together?

Communicative Activity 2-3B

1. **Situation**   Your partner has a list of things he or she needs to do this weekend and you have a list of things you want to do.

Task   Find out if there are things you might be able to do together by answering your partner's questions and listening to what he or she says. Write down your partner's errands next to your list.

MODELO   A — **Necesito ir al centro comercial. ¿Qué quieres hacer?**
B — **Quiero comprar ropa.**

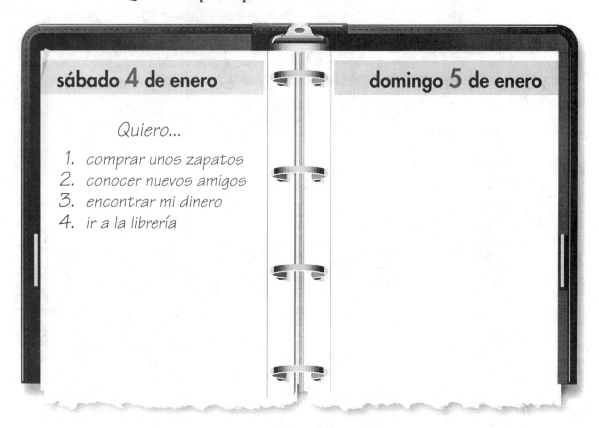

sábado 4 de enero

domingo 5 de enero

Quiero...

1. comprar unos zapatos
2. conocer nuevos amigos
3. encontrar mi dinero
4. ir a la librería

2. Now compare your lists. What will you be able to do together? What won't you be able to do together?

1. **Situation**   Classes start tomorrow morning. You and your partner received each other's class schedules for the new semester by mistake.

Task   Ask your partner for the correct schedule information.

MODELO   A — ¿Qué clase tengo a las ocho y media?
         B — La clase de ciencias.
         A — ¿Cómo se llama el profesor?
         B — Se llama el profesor Macías.

Hora	Clase	Profesor(a)
8:30–9:30	ciencias	el profesor Macías
9:30–10:30		
10:30–10:45	descanso	
10:45–11:45		
11:45–12:15	almuerzo	
12:15–1:15		
1:15–1:30	descanso	
1:30–2:30		
2:30–3:30		

2. Now give your partner the information to fill in his or her schedule.

MODELO   B — ¿Qué clase tengo a las ocho y media?
         A — La clase de francés.
         B — ¿Cómo se llama el profesor?
         A — Se llama la profesora Bermondy.

Hora	Clase	Profesor(a)
8:30–9:30	francés	la profesora Bermondy
9:30–10:30	química	el profesor Peña
10:30–10:45	descanso	
10:45–11:45	coro	el profesor Méndez
11:45–12:15	almuerzo	
12:15–1:15	matemáticas	la profesora Díaz
1:15–1:30	descanso	
1:30–2:30	geografía	la profesora Smith
2:30–3:30	español	el profesor Galindo

What times during the day do your schedules match? _____ _____ _____ _____

Communicative Activity 3-1 B

COMMUNICATIVE ACTIVITIES

1. **Situation** Classes start tomorrow morning. You and your partner received each other's class schedules for the new semester by mistake.

Task Give your partner the correct schedule information.

MODELO   A — ¿Qué clase tengo a las ocho y media?
               B — La clase de ciencias.
               A — ¿Cómo se llama el profesor?
               B — Se llama el profesor Macías

Hora	Clase	Profesor(a)
8:30–9:30	ciencias	el profesor Macías
9:30–10:30	arte	la profesora Rodríguez
10:30–10:45	descanso	
10:45–11:45	inglés	el profesor García
11:45–12:15	almuerzo	
12:15–1:15	matemáticas	la profesora Díaz
1:15–1:30	descanso	
1:30–2:30	español	el profesor Galindo
2:30–3:30	ciencias sociales	el profesor Pérez

2. Now ask your partner for the information to fill in your schedule.

MODELO   B — ¿Qué clase tengo a las ocho y media?
               A — La clase de francés.
               B — ¿Cómo se llama el profesor?
               A — Se llama la profesora Bermondy.

Hora	Clase	Profesor(a)
8:30–9:30	francés	la profesora Bermondy
9:30–10:30		
10:30–10:45	descanso	
10:45–11:45		
11:45–12:15	almuerzo	
12:15–1:15		
1:15–1:30	descanso	
1:30–2:30		
2:30–3:30		

What times during the day do your schedules match? _____ _____ _____ _____

¡Ven conmigo! Adelante Level 1A, Chapter 3

1. **Situation**   You're staying in Cuernavaca for a week with your family. You call your partner to find out about some of the events that are going on in town.

Task   Your partner has a local entertainment guide and you have a newspaper. Some of the events listed are the same, but your newspaper has some missing information. Look at the schedule below and ask your partner for the information you need.

MODELO   A — ¿A qué hora es la clase de computación?
                      B — Es a las seis y media.

1. _____

_____

2. _____

_____

2. Now answer your partner's questions about the following ads.

Which two events take place at the same time? _____

Communicative Activity 3-2B

1. **Situation**   You live in Cuernavaca. Your partner is visiting from the United States and wants to find out about things to do in town for the week.

Task   Your partner has a newspaper and you have a local entertainment guide. Some of the events listed are the same, but your entertainment guide has more complete information. Look at the schedule below and answer your partner's questions.

MODELO   A — ¿A qué hora es la clase de computación?
　　　　　B — Es a las seis y media.

2. Now switch roles and ask your partner about the following ads.

1. _____
_____

2. _____
_____

3. _____
_____

Which two events take place at the same time? _____

Communicative Activity 3-3A

1. Situation You and your partner are arranging photos of the new teachers for the yearbook.

Task Ask your partner what each teacher on your list is like. Match the names to the photos according to your partner's description. You have photos of Sra. Alvarado, Sr. Dávila, Srta. Camacho, Sr. Carrillo, Sra. Franco, and Sr. González.

MODELO A — ¿Cómo es la Sra. Alvarado?
B — Es alta, rubia e inteligente.

_____ _____ _____

Sra. Alvarado

_____ _____ _____

2. Now answer your partner's questions to match her or his photos with the correct name.

MODELO B — ¿Cómo es el Sr. García?
A — Es alto, moreno y estricto.

NOMBRE	¿CÓMO ES?
Sr. Gutiérrez	alto, rubio, guapo, simpático
Srta. Guzmán	alta, bonita, morena, cómica
Sra. Benavides	rubia, simpática, interesante
Sr. Romero	bajo, moreno, guapo, aburrido
Sra. Fernández	baja, rubia, inteligente
Sr. García	alto, moreno, estricto, antipático

Which teachers' classes would you most enjoy? _____ and _____.

Why? _____

Communicative Activity 3-3B

COMMUNICATIVE ACTIVITIES

1. **Situation** You and your partner are arranging photos of the new teachers for the yearbook.

Task Answer your partner's questions to match his or her photos with the correct name.

MODELO   A — ¿Cómo es la Sra. Alvarado?
           B — Es alta, rubia e inteligente.

NOMBRE	¿CÓMO ES?
Sra. Alvarado	alta, rubia, inteligente
Sr. Dávila	alto, moreno, guapo, estricto
Sr. Carrillo	bajo, rubio, cómico
Srta. Camacho	alta, morena, simpática
Sra. Franco	alta, morena, antipática, estricta
Sr. González	bajo, moreno, simpático, cómico

2. Now ask your partner what each teacher on your list is like. Match the names to the photos according to your partner's description. You have photos of Sr. Gutiérrez, Srta. Guzmán, Sra. Benavides, Sr. Romero, Sra. Fernández, and Sr. García.

MODELO   B — ¿Cómo es el Sr. García?
           A — Es alto, moreno y estricto.

Sr. García
_____

_____

_____

_____

_____

_____

Which teachers' classes would you most enjoy? _____ and _____.

Why? _____

¡Ven conmigo! Adelante Level 1A, Chapter 3

Nombre _____ Clase _____ Fecha _____

1. **Situation**   You and your partner are working on the school newspaper. You both have been assigned to interview a number of new exchange students, so you've split up the interviews.

Task   Ask your partner questions about his or her interviews to complete the article for the paper.

MODELO   A — ¿Qué le gusta hacer a Julio?
B — A Julio le gusta montar en bicicleta. También le gusta...

Julio	Martín	José Luis
montar en bicicleta		

2. Now help your partner by sharing the information you have from your interviews.

MODELO   B — ¿Qué le gusta hacer a Amelia?
A — A Amelia le gusta ir a fiestas. También le gusta...

Amelia	Guadalupe	Lorena
ir a fiestas	escuchar música	practicar deportes
pasar el rato con amigos	pintar	hablar con amigos
caminar en el parque	nadar	escuchar música
escuchar música	tocar el piano	montar en bicicleta

How many of the students enjoy music? _____ swimming? _____ painting? _____

Which activity is the most popular? _____

Communicative Activity 4-1 B

1. **Situation** You and your partner are working on the school newspaper. You both have been assigned to interview a number of new exchange students, so you've split up the interviews.

   Task Answer your partner's questions about your interviews to complete the article for the paper.

   MODELO
   A — ¿Qué le gusta hacer a Julio?
   B — A Julio le gusta montar en bicicleta. También le gusta...

Julio	Martín	José Luis
montar en bicicleta	toca la guitarra	ir a fiestas
pasar el rato con amigos	pintar	escuchar música
practicar deportes	practicar deportes	caminar en el parque
nadar	escuchar música	pasar el rato con amigos

2. Now ask your partner questions to get the information he or she has from the interviews.

   MODELO
   B — ¿Qué le gusta hacer a Amelia?
   A — A Amelia le gusta ir a fiestas. También le gusta...

Amelia	Guadalupe	Lorena
ir a fiestas		

How many of the students enjoy music? _____ swimming? _____ painting? _____

Which activity is the most popular? _____

1. **Situation**   Your partner borrowed several of your things. He or she returned them to your room, but you can't find them because they're not where they belong.

Task   Ask your partner where each of these things is and mark each one on the drawing of your room according to what your partner tells you.

MODELO   A — ¿Dónde está mi diccionario?
B — Está debajo de la cama.

libro de francés
diccionario   videojuego
radio

2. Now switch roles. Answer your partner's questions according to this drawing.

MODELO   B — ¿Dónde está mi mochila?
A — Está debajo de la cama.

Compare your answers to be sure you each marked the items as they appear in the drawings.

Communicative Activity 4-2B

1. **Situation** You borrowed several of your partner's things. You returned them to your partner's room, but he or she can't find them because they're not where they belong.

Task Answer your partner's questions according to the drawing.

MODELO   A — ¿Dónde está mi diccionario?
           B — Está debajo de la cama.

2. Now switch roles. Ask your partner where he or she put these things. Mark each one on the drawing of your room.

MODELO   B — ¿Dónde está mi mochila?
           A — Está debajo de la cama.

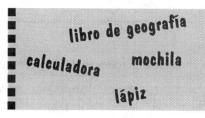

libro de geografía

calculadora   mochila

lápiz

Compare your answers to be sure you each marked the items as they appear in the drawings.

Nombre _____ Clase _____ Fecha _____

1. **Situation** You and your partner are secret agents trying to crack a suspected spy ring. You've followed a man with the codename "**Liebre**". Your partner has followed a woman codenamed "**Ardilla**".

Task Ask your partner for the information he or she has obtained on "**Ardilla**". If there is a day for which your partner doesn't have information, put an X in the blank.

MODELO   A — ¿Adónde va "Ardilla" los martes?
          B — Los martes a las seis de la tarde va al supermercado.

Las actividades de Ardilla		
día	hora	¿adónde va?
los lunes		
los martes	6:00 P.M.	al supermercado
los miércoles		
los jueves		
los viernes		
los sábados		
los domingos		

2. Now answer your partner's questions about "**Liebre**" according to these photos. If there is a day for which you don't have a photo, tell your partner, "**No sé.**"

MODELO   B — ¿Adónde va Liebre los lunes?
          A — Los lunes a las ocho de la mañana va a la piscina.

los lunes, 8 a.m.

los domingos, 9:30 a.m.

los jueves, 7:30 p.m.

los sábados, 4 p.m.

los martes, 1 p.m.

los miércoles, 6 p.m.

Is there a time and place during the week the two suspects might be meeting to exchange

information?_____

Communicative Activity 4-3B

1. **Situation** You and your partner are secret agents trying to crack a suspected spy ring. You've followed a woman with the codename "**Ardilla**". Your partner has followed a man codenamed "**Liebre**".

Task Answer your partner's questions about "**Ardilla**" according to these photos. If there is a day for which you don't have a photo, tell your partner, "**No sé.**"

MODELO A — ¿Adónde va "Ardilla" los martes?
  B — Los martes a las seis de la tarde va al supermercado.

los sábados, 4 p.m.

los miércoles, 7:30 p.m.

los viernes, 8 p.m.

los jueves, 2 p.m.

los domingos, 9:30 a.m.

los martes, 6 p.m.

2. Now ask your partner for the information he or she has obtained on "**Liebre**". If there is a day for which your partner doesn't have information, put an X in the blank.

MODELO B — ¿Adónde va Liebre los lunes?
  A — Los lunes a las ocho de la mañana va a la piscina.

Las actividades de Liebre		
día	**hora**	**¿adónde va?**
los lunes	8:00 A.M.	a la piscina
los martes		
los miércoles		
los jueves		
los viernes		
los sábados		
los domingos		

Is there a time and place during the week the two suspects might be meeting to exchange

information? _____

¡Ven conmigo! Adelante Level 1A, Chapter 4

Communicative Activity 5-1 A

1. Situation   You and your partner have just completed a survey for your PE class on the health habits of 100 students in your school.

Task   Ask your partner for the information she or he has compiled from the survey. Fill in the chart with the numbers your partner gives you.

MODELO   A — ¿Cuántos estudiantes nunca asisten a una clase de
            ejercicios aeróbicos?
         B — Veintisiete estudiantes.
         A — ¿Y a veces?
         B — Cuarenta y tres estudiantes.
         A — ¿Y todos los días?
         B — Treinta estudiantes.

	nunca	a veces	todos los días
asistir a una clase de ejercicios aeróbicos	27	43	30
comer ensalada			
correr dos millas			
tomar refrescos			
practicar un deporte			

2. Now help your partner complete the chart by answering his or her questions. Use the information you've compiled below.

MODELO   B — ¿Cuántos estudiantes nunca comen hamburguesas
            con papas fritas?
         A — Diez estudiantes.
         B — ¿Y a veces?
         A — Sesenta y cuatro estudiantes.
         B — ¿Y todos los días?
         A — Veintiséis estudiantes.

	nunca	a veces	todos los días
comer hamburguesas con papas fritas	10	64	26
desayunar	2	79	19
comer frutas	5	80	15
mirar mucha televisión	11	25	64
caminar	2	10	88

Now compare both charts. Which activity do most students participate in every day? _____

Sometimes? _____ Never? _____

Nombre _____ Clase _____ Fecha _____

 Communicative Activity 5-1B

COMMUNICATIVE ACTIVITIES

1. **Situation**   You and your partner have just completed a survey for your PE class on the health habits of 100 students in your school.

Task   Help your partner complete the chart by answering his or her questions. Use the information you've compiled below.

MODELO   A — ¿Cuántos estudiantes nunca asisten a una clase de
                      ejercicios aeróbicos?
              B — Veintisiete estudiantes.
              A — ¿Y a veces?
              B — Cuarenta y tres estudiantes.
              A — ¿Y todos los días?
              B — Treinta estudiantes.

	nunca	a veces	todos los días
asistir a una clase de ejercicios aeróbicos	27	43	30
comer ensalada	18	71	11
correr dos millas	63	28	9
tomar refrescos	14	49	37
practicar un deporte	19	47	34

2. Now switch roles. Ask your partner for the information he or she has compiled from the survey. Fill in the chart with the numbers your partner gives you.

MODELO   B — ¿Cuántos estudiantes nunca comen hamburguesas con papas fritas?
              A — Diez estudiantes.
              B — ¿Y a veces?
              A — Sesenta y cuatro estudiantes.
              B — ¿Y todos los días?
              A — Veintiséis estudiantes.

	nunca	a veces	todos los días
comer hamburguesas con papas fritas	10	64	26
desayunar			
comer frutas			
mirar mucha televisión			
caminar			

Compare both charts. Which activity do the most students participate in every day? _____

Sometimes? _____ Never? _____

¡Ven conmigo! Adelante Level 1A, Chapter 5

Nombre _____ Clase _____ Fecha _____

1. **Situation**   You and your partner both live in Miami. You both have friends visiting over the holiday break. You want to invite both groups of friends to do various activities.

Task   Ask your partner which activities his or her guests like. Mark each one in the chart below.

MODELO   A — ¿Qué le gusta a Roberto?
             B — Le gusta nadar.
             A — ¿Le gusta nadar a Lola?
             B — No, no le gusta nadar pero le gusta leer novelas.

	nadar	bucear	leer novelas	esquiar	jugar a un deporte	pescar
Roberto	X					
Lola			X			
Graciela						
Melisa						
Alejandro						
Luis						

2. Now answer your partner's questions about the other guests according to the pictures below.

MODELO   B — ¿Qué le gusta a Mariana?
             A — Le gusta correr.
             B — ¿Le gusta correr a Gregorio?
             A — No, no le gusta correr pero le gusta ir a bailes.

   Mariana   **Gregorio**   **Isabel**   **Carlos**   **Raquel**   **Esteban**

How many of all the guests seem to prefer active pastimes? _____

Communicative Activity 5-2B

1. **Situation**   You and your partner both live in Miami. You both have friends visiting over the holiday break. You want to invite both groups of friends to do various activities.

Task   Answer your partner's questions about which activities his or her guests like to do according to the drawings below.

MODELO   A — ¿Qué le gusta a Roberto?
B — Le gusta nadar.
A — ¿Le gusta nadar a Lola?
B — No, no le gusta nadar pero le gusta leer novelas.

| Roberto | Lola | Graciela | Melisa | Alejandro | Luis |

2. Now ask your partner about her or his guests' favorite activities. Mark the information in the chart below.

MODELO   B — ¿Qué le gusta a Mariana?
A — Le gusta correr.
B — ¿Le gusta correr a Gregorio?
A — No, no le gusta correr pero le gusta ir a bailes.

	acampar	hacer ejercico	correr	descansar	escribir tarjetas postales	ir a bailes
Mariana			X			
Gregorio						X
Isabel						
Carlos						
Raquel						
Esteban						

How many of all the guests seem to prefer active pastimes? _____

Nombre _____ Clase _____ Fecha _____

1. **Situation** You and your partner are writing a travel column for your local newspaper. Your readers will want to know about the weather in different areas of the U.S.

Task Ask your partner about the weather in each of the following cities. Fill in the chart with the information he or she gives you.

MODELO A — ¿Qué tiempo hace en Omaha en enero?
        B — Está nublado y nieva mucho.

Ciudad	enero	julio
Omaha	está nublado nieva mucho	
St. Louis		
Dallas		
Denver		
Indianapolis		

2. Now answer your partner's questions about the weather in each of the following cities. Use the information you have in the chart below.

MODELO B — ¿Qué tiempo hace en Olympia en julio?
        A — Hace sol y hace viento.

Ciudad	enero	julio
Olympia	🌧️	☀️ 💨
Seattle	🌧️	☀️ 🌧️
Portland	🌧️	☁️
Boise	❄️	☁️
San Francisco	☁️ 🌡️ 30° F	💨 ☁️

In which cities would you need to carry an umbrella in the winter? _____

Which cities have the most similar weather in July? _____

Communicative Activity 5-3B

1. **Situation**   You and your partner are writing a travel column for your local newspaper. Your readers will want to know about the weather in different areas of the U.S.

Task   Answer your partner's questions about the weather in each of the following cities. Use the information you have in the chart below.

MODELO   A — ¿Qué tiempo hace en Omaha en enero?
    B — Está nublado y nieva mucho.

Ciudad	enero	julio
Omaha		
St. Louis		
Dallas		
Denver		
Indianapolis		

2. Now ask your partner about the weather in each of the following cities. Fill in the chart with the information she or he gives you.

MODELO   B — ¿Qué tiempo hace en Olympia en julio?
    A — Hace sol y hace viento.

Ciudad	enero	julio
Olympia		hace sol y viento
Seattle		
Portland		
Boise		
San Francisco		

In which cities would you need to carry an umbrella in the winter?_____

Which cities have the most similar weather in July?_____

Communicative Activity 6-1A

1. **Situation**   You and your partner are distant cousins collecting information for your entire family tree. You each have all the information about one family, but only some of the information about the other.

Task   Ask your partner questions that will help you fill in the missing family names for the Santos family.

MODELO   A — ¿Quién es la hermana de Elena?
         B — La hermana de Elena es Julia.

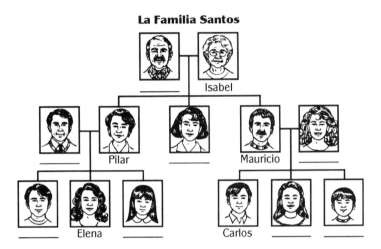

La Familia Santos

Isabel

Pilar   Mauricio

Elena   Carlos

2. Now answer your partner's questions about the Reyes family.

MODELO   B — ¿Quién es el esposo de Rosa?
         A — El esposo de Rosa es Julio.

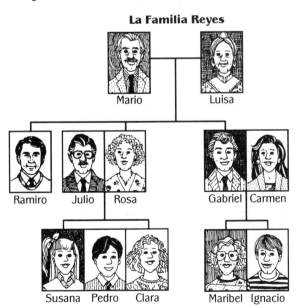

La Familia Reyes

Mario   Luisa

Ramiro   Julio   Rosa   Gabriel   Carmen

Susana   Pedro   Clara   Maribel   Ignacio

Compare your completed family trees. How are the Santos and the Reyes families related?

Communicative Activity 6-1 B

1. **Situation** You and your partner are distant cousins collecting information for your entire family tree. You each have all the information about one family, but only some of the information about the other.

Task Answer your partner's questions about the Santos family.

MODELO A — ¿Quién es la hermana de Elena?
B — La hermana de Elena es Julia.

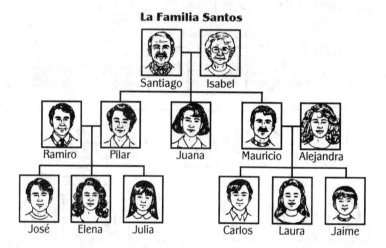

La Familia Santos

2. Now ask your partner for the missing names in the Reyes family.

MODELO B — ¿Quién es el esposo de Rosa?
A — El esposo de Rosa es Julio.

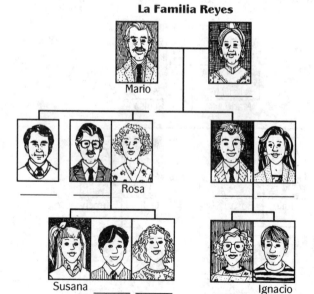

La Familia Reyes

Compare your completed family trees. How are the Santos and the Reyes families related?

_____

Nombre _____ Clase _____ Fecha _____

1. Situation You and your partner have just finished your first day in a new school, and you are comparing notes about your new classmates.

Task Your partner has only some of the information in the following chart. Without saying the student's name, read the list of characteristics for each student. Your partner will fill in the blanks on her or his chart and then guess the student's name.

MODELO A — Esta persona tiene pelo negro, ojos negros, no es ni alto ni
        bajo y es delgado.
        B — ¿Es Rogelio?
        A — Sí, es Rogelio.

Rogelio	Encarnación	Manrique	Mercedes
pelo negro	rubia	pelo castaño	pelirroja
ojos negros	ojos de color café	ojos azules	ojos verdes
ni alto ni bajo	alta	alto	baja
delgado	no delgada	no delgado	delgada

2. Now, talk about what each person is like. You find that your partner has focused on their good qualities, while you saw only the negative ones. Tell your partner what you think of each person, and fill in the blanks with what he or she has to add.

MODELO B — ¿Cómo es Víctor?
        A — Bueno, es egoísta.
        B — Pero también es romántico y atlético.

	Víctor	Silvia	Rosa	Juan Carlos
Good Qualities	romántico atlético			
Bad Qualities	egoísta	aburrida	perezosa	desorganizado

Which person do you think is most interesting? _____

Why? _____

_____

HRW material copyrighted under notice appearing earlier in this work.

Communicative Activity 6-2B

1. **Situation**   You and your partner have just finished your first day in a new school, and you are comparing notes about your new classmates. Your partner remembers more about each student than you do.

Task   Listen while your partner describes a student. Try to guess who your partner is talking about. Fill in the blanks before trying to guess.

MODELO   A — **Esta persona tiene pelo negro, ojos negros, no es ni alto ni bajo y es delgado.**
              B — **¿Es Rogelio?**
              A — **Sí, es Rogelio.**

Rogelio	Encarnación	Manrique	Mercedes
pelo negro		pelo castaño	
ojos negros		ojos azules	ojos verdes
ni alto ni bajo	alta		baja
delgado	no delgada		

2. Now, talk about what each person is like. You find that your partner has focused on their negative qualities, while you saw the good ones. Fill in the blanks with what your partner says about each person; then try to set him or her straight!

MODELO   B — **¿Cómo es Víctor?**
              A — **Bueno, es egoísta.**
              B — **Pero también es romántico y atlético.**

	Víctor	Silvia	Rosa	Juan Carlos
Good Qualities	romántico, atlético	trabajadora, responsable	leal, generosa	artístico, creativo
Bad Qualities	egoísta			

Which person do you think is most interesting? _____

Why? _____

_____

Nombre _____ Clase _____ Fecha _____

1. **Situation**   You have asked your friends to help you with the chores so you can all attend a party together. Your partner has helped you organize the chores into an upstairs list and a downstairs and outside list.

Task   Fill in the chart below by asking your partner what each of your friends should do upstairs.

MODELO   A — ¿Qué debe hacer Santiago?
         B — Santiago debe hacer la cama.

Arriba...   *(Upstairs)*

NOMBRE	Santiago	Alicia	Oralia	Jaime	Eduardo
QUEHACER	debe hacer la cama				

2. Now answer your partner's questions about which downstairs and outside task each of your friends should do.

MODELO   B — ¿Qué debe hacer Orieta?
         A — Orieta debe poner la mesa.

Abajo y afuera...   *(Downstairs and outside)*

NOMBRE	Orieta	Beatriz	Roberto	Rosana	Enrique
QUEHACER	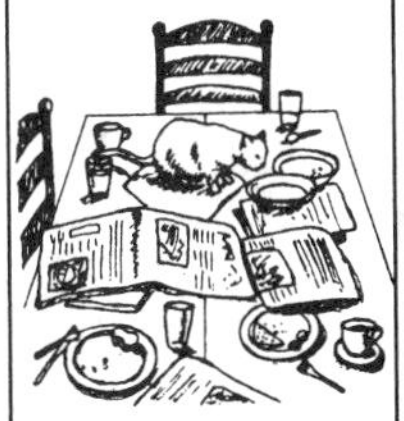	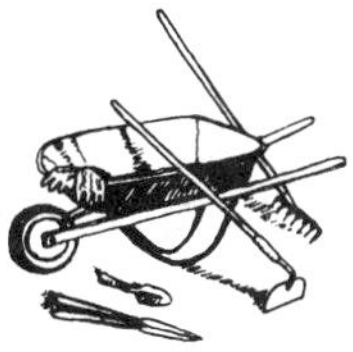	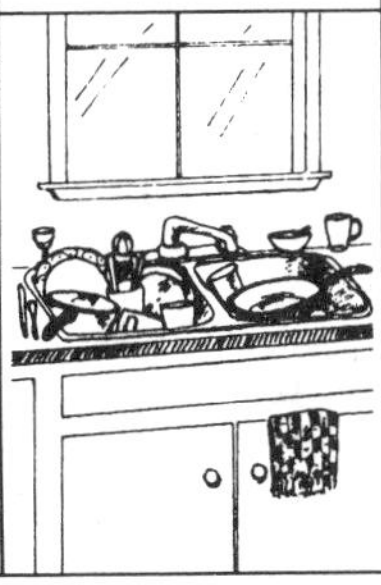	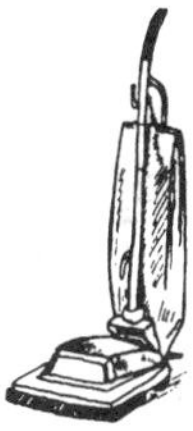	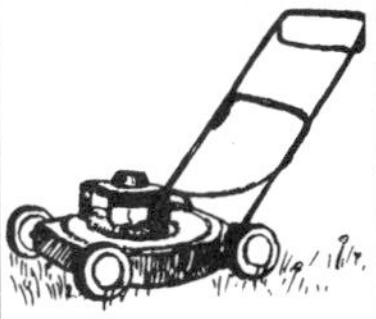

Which friends need to share equipment to finish their chores? _____

and _____

Communicative Activity 6-3B

1. **Situation** You have asked your friends to help you with the chores so you can all attend a party together. Your partner has helped you organize the chores into an upstairs list and a downstairs and outside list.

Task Answer your partner's questions about which upstairs task each of your friends should do.

MODELO   A — ¿Qué debe hacer Santiago?
B — Santiago debe hacer la cama.

Arriba... *(Upstairs)*

NOMBRE	Santiago	Alicia	Oralia	Jaime	Eduardo
QUEHACER					

2. Now, to fill in the chart below, ask your partner which downstairs and outside task each of your friends should do.

MODELO   B — ¿Qué debe hacer Orieta?
A — Orieta debe poner la mesa.

Abajo y afuera... *(Downstairs and outside)*

NOMBRE	Orieta	Beatriz	Roberto	Rosana	Enrique
QUEHACER	debe poner la mesa				

Which friends need to share equipment to finish their chores? _____

and _____

Realia

Realia 1-1

Adapted text and photo from *Ragazza*, no. 91, May 1997. Copyright © 1997 by **Ragazza**. Reprinted by permission of the publisher.

Librería Siglo de Oro

VENTA Y COMPRA
TODO TIPO DE LIBROS
BIBLIOTECAS

- Mapas antiguos
- Postales antiguas
- Fotografías antiguas
- Documentos antiguos
- Cómics, etc.

Alfonso el Sabio, 42
SANTIAGO DE COMPOSTELA
☎ 56 87 32

Retratos Artísticos

Lucinda Aguirre
FOTÓGRAFA PROFESIONAL

CAMARAS Y FOTOS, S.A.
23 Poniente 2345   Tel. 42-87-22   Monterrey, NL

CHOCOLATES
LA GALLEGA, S.A.

José María Lado Ochoa

15004 LA CORUÑA
Cuatrocaminos, 8 - Teléf. 22 11 23
Particular 23 35 21 - 65 32 48

Viajes extraordinarios
Sus Asesores en Viajes Desde 1963

Juan E. Benavides
Ejecutivo de Ventas

Tel.: (506) 22-22-55 • Fax: (506) 31-9233
Paseo Colón, 231 • Apdo. 4837 - 1000
San José, Costa Rica

REALIA

Realia 1-3

SOLICITUD DE PASAPORTE

radical	NUMERO	ANO

FOTOS

CLASE	SERIE	NUMERO
☐ I ☐ E ☐ C		

excmo. SENOR:

TITULAR

NOMBRE	APELLIDO 1	*ROMERO*
ROSA MARIA	APELLIDO 2	*BARREIRO*

D.N.I.	SEXO	PROFESION	ESTADO CIVIL
33.260.717	*F*		*SOLTERA*

LUGAR DE NACIMIENTO	PROVINCIA NACIMIENTO	CLAVE	F. NACIMIENTO
SANTIAGO	*LA CORUÑA*		*28. X .87*

NOMBRE DEL PADRE	NOMBRE DE LA MADRE
VENTURA	*MARIA*

DOMICILIO

CALLE O PLAZA	Nº	D.P.
EDUARDO PONDAL	*24*	

LOCALIDAD	PROVINCIA	CLAVE
SANTIAGO	*LA CORUÑA*	

SOLICITUD DE PASAPORTE

radical	NUMERO	ANO

fotos

CLASE	SERIE	NUMERO
☐ I ☐ E ☐ C		

excmo. SENOR:

TITULAR

nombre	APELLIDO 1	
	APELLIDO 2	

D.N.I.	SEXO	PROFESION	ESTADO CIVIL

LUGAR DE NACIMIENTO	PROVINCIA NACIMIENTO	CLAVE	F. NACIMIENTO

NOMBRE DEL PADRE	NOMBRE DE LA MADRE

DOMICILIO

CALLE O PLAZA	Nº	D.P.

LOCALIDAD	PROVINCIA	CLAVE

¡Ven conmigo! Adelante Level 1A, Chapter 1

Realia 1-1: Fotonovela advertisement

1. **Reading:** Have students look at the photograph for clues about what might be going on in the scene. Is Cristián happy to be speaking to Clara? How do they know?

2. **Listening:** Read the dialogue out loud, changing your voice for the different characters and ask students to identify the speaker (Clara or Cristián).

3. **Writing:** Have students write a similar dialogue that might take place when you call a friend or receive a call from a friend.

4. **Pair work/Speaking:** Have students act out the dialogue or the one that they wrote for number 3.

Realia 1-2: Business cards

1. **Reading:** Have students read over the business cards paying special attention to graphics and cognates. What types of businesses are represented?

2. **Writing:** Have students list the names of the people whose cards these are and identify the names of the companies they work for.

3. **Speaking:** Give students different situations and ask students whom they would call to have certain things done, for example, to have a family photo made, or to plan a vacation, or to order custom-made chocolates for a party.

4. **Group work/Speaking:** Divide students into groups of two or three. Have students choose an identity for themselves from the business cards and role-play introductions.

5. **Reading:** Have students look over the cards. What do they like and not like about each card? What would they change about the cards to make them more interesting or eye-catching? Have students design their own cards for any business they choose.

REALIA

Using Realia 1-2, 1-3

Realia 1-3: Passport applications

1. **Speaking:** Ask students what this form is for. Why might someone need a passport?

2. **Listening:** Tell students that this passport application is from Spain. You may want to go over with students the meaning of any unfamiliar terms: **apellido 1, apellido 2, D.N.I., estado civil, provincia de nacimiento, nº, localidad,** and **provincia.** Remind students that a Spanish speaker's first **apellido** comes from the father and the second comes from the mother. **D.N.I.** stands for **documento nacional de identidad,** the Spanish equivalent of a Social Security card. Spain is divided into regions and provinces (**provincias**) instead of states and counties; **nº** is the Spanish abbreviation for **número**; and **localidad** means *town* or *city*.

3. **Reading:** Have students read the information on the filled-out application and give five facts about the applicant.

4. **Writing:** Have students fill out the blank application or supply the information on a blank sheet of paper. They may use the completed application as a guide.

5. **Group work/Speaking:** Divide the class into groups of two or three. Have students ask one another questions and use the information to fill out the blank form.

REALIA

En Alberto los precios son lo mejor

30% DESCUENTO

Mochila U.S. Army

Antes....*1.995*   Ahora.....*1.395*

30% DESCUENTO

Bolígrafos Micro bandera

Antes....*2.195*   Ahora.....*1.500*

Juego de útiles escolares
495

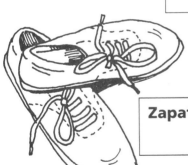

Deportes Class
4595

Zapatillas class
850

R E A L I A

---

20 CENTROS ALBERTO

Alberto

VIGO 1
POL INDUSTRIAL DE COIA
Av. Caseloo. S/n. Parc. 200

VIGO 2
Avda. Madrid

LA CORUÑA
Av. Alcalde Alfonso Molina
Palavea

Ferrol
Polígono industrial
Ensenada de la Gándara

GIJON
Ctra. Nac.630, km 487
Roces

UTEBO
Ctra. Zaragoza-
Logroño, km 13

LOGROÑO
Camino de la Tejera, s/n

S. QUIRZE DEL VALLES
Autopista A-12
Salida SABADELL Norte

 Bar cafetería
Restaurante

 Información
General

 Todos los
servicios
En electro-
domésticos

 Servicio transporte
Para electro-
domésticos

 Parking
Gratuito

 Horario de 10 a 22 h. Lunes
a sábado y domingos,
Vaguada, Leganes y Alcalá
de Henares

Realia 2-2

Advertisement from Mueblerías Berrios, June 1997. Reprinted by permission of *Mueblerías Berrios*.

Using Realia 2-1, 2-2

Realia 2-1: School supply ad

1. **Reading/Speaking:** Ask students about the prices in the ad. How do the prices compare to the cost of those items in the United States? Explain to students that the prices shown are in **pesetas**, the currency of Spain. Have students look up the exchange rate for the **peseta** in a newspaper and convert the prices to dollars. Are the items advertised expensive, inexpensive, or comparably priced to similar items where you live? Ask students if the items advertised are items they would buy.

2. **Reading:** Ask students to scan the ad for cognates and list them on the chalk-board or overhead projector. Then ask them what they think the small graphics at the bottom of the advertisement represent. If they don't guess correctly, tell them what services these graphics represent.

3. **Group work/Writing:** Have students work in groups and create their own school supply ad. Bring in advertisements and have students cut out items and write the text to accompany each item in Spanish. Have them assign realistic prices in **pesetas**.

Realia 2-2: Bedroom furniture ad

1. **Speaking:** Ask students ¿**Qué hay en el cuarto?** Have them identify the different items in the ad using the vocabulary they have learned in this chapter (**silla, cama, lámpara, ventana, escritorio,** etc.)

2. **Reading:** Have students scan the ad for cognates and list them on the chalkboard or on an overhead transparency. Encourage students to guess the meanings of the words based on the context. Explain any unfamiliar words. Point out to students that since this ad is from Puerto Rico, English words are mixed in with the Spanish, as is often the case in informal contexts. Ask students how many different payment plans the store offers.

3. **Writing:** Have students write their own ads for a furniture store featuring what they would have in their ideal rooms. Have them include prices.

4. **Speaking:** Have students present their ads to the class in the style of a television commercial for a furniture store or of a feature on a celebrity home. They should describe the contents of the room and say how many they have of certain pieces of furniture.

Realia 2-3: Back to school ad

1. **Reading:** Have students look at the ad to figure out what is being advertised. What clues tell them that this is an ad for back to school supplies (after the Christmas break, which usually lasts about a month in many South American countries)?

2. **Speaking:** Tell students **Hoy es el primer día de clases.** Then ask individuals **¿Qué necesitas hacer?** Have them look at the ad to get ideas (**comprar ropa, ir a la librería,** etc.)

3. **Writing:** Have students write a list of things they need to do before the first day of classes after a long break. Tell them to imagine that they need to have some of the same things as the students in the ad. What will they need to buy?

4. **Pair work/Speaking:** Have students work in pairs to create one list of things to buy and do before school starts that they can both agee on and then present their list to the class.

¡Ven conmigo! Adelante Level 1A, Chapter 2   Activities for Communication   **47**

HRW material copyrighted under notice appearing earlier in this work.

Secundaria Benito Juárez

Avenida del Charro No. 523 Sur
Cd. Juárez, Chih. México
Tels. 23-28-45 y 15-45-90

Horario de Clases del Turno Matutino
Alumno: Martínez López, Juan Ramón

2do. Año B
1998–1999

HORA	LUNES	MARTES	MIÉRCOLES	JUEVES	VIERNES
8:00 – 8:50	ESPAÑOL	ESPAÑOL	CÓMPUTO	ESPAÑOL	ESPAÑOL
9:00 – 9:50	C. SOCIALES	C. NATURALES	CÓMPUTO	C. SOCIALES	C. NATURALES
10:00 –10:50	C. SOCIALES	C. NATURALES	CÓMPUTO	C. SOCIALES	C. NATURALES
11:00 –11:50	MATÉMATICAS	LÓGICA	MATÉMATICAS	MATÉMATICAS	MATÉMATICAS
12:20 – 1:10	RECESO	RECESO	RECESO	RECESO	RECESO
1:20 – 2:10	ED. FÍSICA	INGLÉS	INGLÉS	LÓGICA	INGLÉS
2:20 – 3:10	ED. FÍSICA	MATÉMATICAS	ESPAÑOL	LAB. C. NAT	LAB. C. NAT

Nota: Las clases darán inicio el lunes 7 de septiembre.

HOY EN LA TV
PROGRAMACIÓN

4 de septiembre

CANAL 6

05.30 De madrugada. Comentarios, entrevistas, noticias.

06.30 Aquí, este día. Variedades matutinas, noticias.

09.10 Para desayunar. En la cocina con el chef Gonzalo. Pan francés y canelones.

10.50 Saber soñar. Telenovela. Los chicos de la banda ganan el festival.

11.40 Telediario. Noticias.

13.00 DeporTV. Lo último en el fútbol.

13.40 Fútbol. Garzas vs Caribe Azul.

15.40 Todo por tu cariño. Telenovela. Mariana pierde a su hijo en la estación del metro.

17.10 El tiempo.

17.30 Cine. *Cuando cantan los lagartos*. Película mexicana.

20.00 Caricaturas. El Príncipe Galáctico.

20.30 ¡Rockhora! Videos.

21.30 XX Festival de la Canción Moderna. 30 países participan.

23.55 Último Saludo. La última información del día.

CANAL 10

05.00 El nuevo sol. Noticias y Variedades con Yvonne Mercado.

08.00 Un día especial. Programa infantil.

10.00 Brincando la cuerda. Programa de ejercicios matutinos con Rebeca Cuni.

12.05 Al mediodía. Noticias.

13.00 Juventina. Telenovela. Juventina riñe con Leonardo. Pedro recibe una carta de España.

13.30 La noche triste. Telenovela histórica. Cortez desembarca en México.

14.00 Rescate en Malibú. Teleserie. El tiburón.

15.00 En color de rosa. Teleserie. Amanda pierde la agencia de publicidad.

16.00 Te recuerdo. Telenovela. Javier confiesa a Alejandra que él es el admirador secreto.

17.00 El chico del 12. Programa de diversiones.

REALIA

Realia 3-3

LOS CHICOS DE LA TELE

Las nuevas caras de la televisión son alegres, simpáticas y juveniles. Las vemos todos los días en nuestras casas pero todavía no las conocemos bien. Aquí te presentamos a tres. Estamos seguros de que todos serán grandes estrellas. ¡Suerte, chicos!

MARKO SANTANDER PUIG

Tiene cara de ángel. Es rubio y de ojos azules. Lo vemos todas las tardes en "Cazadores del Tiempo". Marko nació en Buenos Aires e hizo su primera película a los siete años, su madre es una conocida cantante europea. Adora el fútbol y practica baloncesto todos los días. "Soy muy tímido", dice, pero nosotros no le creemos. ¡Es guapísimo!

GRACIELA RODLÁN ALLENDE

Es superatlética! Sus amigos la llaman la mujer dinamita, nunca para. Graciela es una morena que cursa el primer año de secundaria. Lo que más le gusta es actuar en la televisión. Es famosa por su participación en la teleserie "Muñecas, Muñecas" (Canal 4). Su chico ideal—¿listos?—son los morochos de ojos oscuros.

JORGE ALEJANDRO SAMOS

Es el popular Juan del programa "Siempre de Prisa". En el futuro quiere actuar en una película de Hollywood. "Es un chico muy romántico e inteligente", nos dice su madre. Le gusta mucho el ejercicio, jugar con su perro y leer. "Gasto todo mi dinero en libros y a veces videojuegos", dice.

Realia 3-1: Class schedule

1. **Reading:** Have students read over the schedule paying special attention to new vocabulary and cognates. Ask which classes they can identify by using their knowledge of cognates.

2. **Writing:** Divide the class into groups of four. Have them write a class schedule for a typical week at school.

3. **Group work/Speaking:** Have students practice asking one another what class or classes they have at certain times or on certain days. Ask students to discuss differences between their own class schedules and this one.

Realia 3-2: Television guide

1. **Listening/Speaking:** Read students the time and the channel of specific programs and have them identify the programs.

2. **Reading:** Have students find two or three of each of the following types of programs and tell at what times they're shown:
   news programs
   sporting events
   children's programming
   soap operas (**telenovelas**)

3. **Writing:** Have students choose one news program, one sports event, and one children's program and write out the times at which they are shown.

4. **Pair work/Writing/Speaking:** Have students make a list of three or four programs that interest them. Have them exchange their lists with a partner and ask one another the times of the programs.

5. **Listening/Speaking:** Divide the class into two teams. One student from each team will compete at a time. Give the students the name of the show and the channel it's on. The first student to find the show and say what time it's on gets the point for his or her team.

REALIA

Using Realia 3-3

Realia 3-3: Los chicos de la tele

1. **Reading:** Ask students to read the article. Tell them to think of context as a clue to help them understand unfamiliar words and phrases. Give them a few examples to help illustrate this point. (**nació, conocida, nunca para**). Ask students to identify cognates. Explain that some words that look like English words may be false cognates (**juveniles** *youthful*).

2. **Speaking:** Based on the reading, ask students how they imagine the personalities of the TV stars to be. Have students tell you which of the three they would like to have as a friend and why.

3. **Group work/Writing:** Divide the class into groups of three or four. Have students write a short paragraph describing themselves as if they were TV personalities. Ask them to select a spokesperson and to help him or her practice in order to prepare an oral report to the class. In the report, the spokesperson should describe each group member but not mention his or her name. Have the rest of the class identify each student being described.

REALIA

LOS ARTISTAS DICEN...

GENTE TOTAL

El ecléctico grupo teatral
Gente Total *tomó unos minutos
del ensayo de la nueva comedia
musical* **Vientos del Sur** *para
contestar nuestra pregunta
de la semana:*

¿Qué **haces** en
tu **tiempo libre?**

♦ **Mitsuko:** con tantos ensayos casi no tengo tiempo para divertirme, pero cuando puedo voy a patinar. ¡Me encanta! Me gusta mucho ir al cine con un buen amigo.

♦ **Juan Carlos:** a mí me gusta volar aeroplanos a control remoto, pero también me doy tiempo para nadar o jugar baloncesto. Los domingos por la tarde me gusta pasear en bicicleta con mi familia.

♦ **Samanta:** ¿tiempo libre, chico? ¿Qué es eso? Con la obra y la escuela no tengo tiempo para nada. Bueno, pero me gustan mucho las telenovelas. ¡Ah! Me encanta contar cuentos a mis hermanitas gemelas. Tengo dos.

♦ **Juana Maribel:** me gusta el motociclismo y escribir poemas. ¡Qué contradicción!

♦ **Rosa Marta:** hablar, hablar y hablar, soy una fanática del teléfono. Pero también me gusta correr, hacer gimnasia o aeróbicos.

♦ **José Arturo:** ahora mismo me dedico a practicar varios deportes, como la natación, el squash y el alpinismo. También me gusta ir a montar a caballo en la finca.

♦ **Raúl:** estudio, porque si no tengo buenas notas no puedo trabajar en la obra. Quiero ser un buen artista así que paso el tiempo libre practicando las canciones de la comedia. Me gusta mucho cantar.

Pasa a la página 56

22

R E A L I A

Realia 4-2

NOCHE DE REYES

Ya es de noche en este pequeño pueblo pero todavía hay gente en la calle. Los Reyes quieren dejar su regalo en la casa de Gabriel. Pero... *1-* ¿Podrías decir cuál es la casa de Gabriel, sabiendo que tiene tres ventanas, techo de tejas, dos columnas en la puerta y una enredadera en el frente?; *2-* ¿Qué camino deben tomar los Reyes para llegar a la casa de Gabriel sin cruzarse con nadie?; *3-* Por la calle hay dos personas exactamente iguales. ¿Cuáles son?; *4-* Todos los círculos contienen una parte de esta escena, menos uno. ¿Cuál?

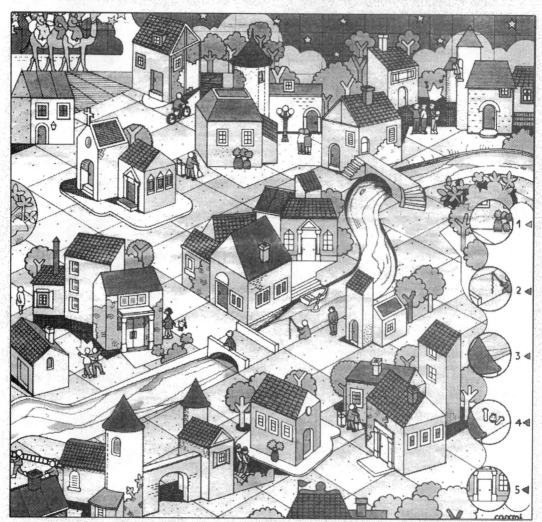

SOLUCIÓN: *1-* Es la de abajo, a la derecha; *2-* Entran por la diagonal, giran a la izquierda, dan vuelta a la manzana de la iglesia, cruzan el puente de escaleras, pasan por detrás de los árboles, pasan bajo el arco y siguen hacia la derecha hasta la casa; *3-* Los dos barrenderos; *4-* El número 4.

nosotros
Ganas de triunfar

Pedro llegará a ser una estrella de rock

Pedro tiene una sonrisa tímida y unas manos enormes que cuando tocan la guitarra se transforman. Aún no sabe qué estilo musical prefiere. De momento, le gusta tocar rock, flamenco y melodías. Quiere componer sus propias canciones por eso estudia solfeo. Sus héroes son Bruce Springsteen y Paco de Lucía. Además de la música le encanta el fútbol. Estas dos aficiones no tienen nada en común pero dice que eso no importa.

Elena sueña con ser una gran bailaora

Elena No pertenece a una familia de artistas pero parece que creció con unos zapatos de tacón en los pies. Le gustaría no hacer otra cosa, sólo bailar. Sus padres piensan que debe estudiar. Ella es joven pero no le falta energía ni talento para llegar a ser una estupenda bailaora. Su sueño es tener algún día su propia compañía de flamenco y viajar por el mundo.

¿Y tú?
¿Qué quieres llegar a ser?

REALIA

Using Realia 4-1, 4-2

Realia 4-1: Gente Total

1. **Reading/Speaking/Group work:** Before showing students the realia, have them brainstorm some things they like to do with their free time. Write some suggestions on the board. Ask students to scan the article looking for cognates. Write them on the board. Explain that **Gente Total** is an acting group formed by teenagers that are also full-time students. Divide students into small groups and assign one or two actors from **Gente Total** to each group. Ask them to read the part of the article that corresponds to their assigned actor. Ask groups to report to the rest of the class what their actors like to do for fun. Ask students if they find the actors' pastimes interesting. Ask them which actor they identify with most.

2. **Speaking:** At random, ask students questions about what they and others like to do. For example: **¿Qué te gusta hacer después de clases? ¿Qué le gusta hacer a Juan Carlos, a Rosa Marta, y a Charlie del grupo Gente Total? ¿Qué le gusta hacer a** (fill in with a classmate's name that has already answer the first question) **después de clases?**

3. **Group work/Writing:** Ask students to discuss in groups which activities they can do in their city and where they can do them. Have students make a brochure explaining the different forms of entertainment that their hometown has to offer.

Realia 4-2: Noche de Reyes

1. **Speaking:** Ask students to look at **Noche de Reyes.** Ask them why they think three men on camels are entering the village on a starry night. Explain that in some parts of Latin America the tradition calls for giving Christmas gifts on January 6.

2. **Reading:** Have students read over and examine **Noche de Reyes** in order to identify buildings, animals and people in general. Ask them to use context to determine the meaning of new vocabulary and to solve the problems/questions given. Use location expressions in order to demonstrate on the map the answers in the **Solución.**

3. **Listening:** Use location expressions from the vocabulary to lead students to a suprise destination in the **Noche de Reyes** city map. You should have determined a location in advance: for example, the castle with the princess in the window. Check to see how many students were able to follow your directions and make it to the correct destination. You may want to ask a few students to select a new secret destination and to give directions to the class on how to get there.

4. **Group work/Speaking:** Divide the class into groups of three or four. Ask them to draw a map of their city, school or neighborhood. Have them use points of reference in order to practice asking and answering questions about the location of people and things on their maps. You may wish to ask spokespersons to present their map and ask the class a few questions.

REALIA

Realia 4-3: Nosotros: Ganas de triunfar

1. **Reading:** Have students read over the article paying special attention to new vocabulary, for example, **componer, transforman, enormes** and **importa**. Help students use cognates and other new vocabulary to come up with at least one question about Elena and Pedro. (Who are Pedro's heroes? What do Elena's parents think she should do?) Ask students to find at least four more facts about Elena and Pedro.

2. **Speaking:** Ask how many students in the class have heard flamenco music or have seen flamenco dancing. If possible, you may wish to play a portion of a flamenco tape or video.

3. **Writing/Pairwork:** Have students work with a partner to create a list of questions that the writer of this article might have asked Elena and Pedro. They should come up with their questions by working back from the information given in the article.

4. **Speaking/Pairwork:** Have students use the questions they compiled in Activity 4 to interview each other.

5. **Writing:** Ask students to write a paragraph about what they do and where they like to go in their free time.

Realia 5-1

REALIA

EL PARADOR
EN EL CORAZÓN DE LA SIERRA TARAHUMARA
24 de junio

Estimada Mesa Directiva del Colegio Juan de la Barrera:
¡Saludos, muchachos! Será un placer contar con su presencia
el fin de semana próximo. Aquí incluimos el calendario de eventos
para los tres días que pasarán en nuestras instalaciones.

¡Los esperamos!

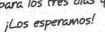

Viernes 28 de junio

8:00 A.M. Bienvenida. Desayuno en el salón Basaseachic.
9:00 A.M. Asignación de dormitorios.
9:30 A.M. Excursión a la laguna "Los patos". Esperamos les guste montar, el viaje a caballo toma dos horas.
4:00 P.M. Clases de tenis.
5:00 P.M. Clases de equitación.
6:00 P.M. Cena en el salón Rarámuri.
7:00 P.M. Fogatada. Canciones y Cuentos alrededor de la fogata.
9:00 P.M. El cine al aire libre exhibirá una película. Churros y chocolate calientito para cuando cae el fresco. Traigan sus cobijas.

Sábado 29 de junio

7:00 A.M. Desayuno. Salón Basaseachic.
8:00 A.M. Inicio del torneo de tenis. El calendario de partidos será anunciado por la mañana. Los partidos son amistosos y duran 45 minutos.

9:00 A.M. Excursión a las Cuevas de Mapimí. Podrán practicar un poco de alpinismo, observarán pinturas rupestres y visitarán una ranchería. Las camionetas salen a las 9, a las 10 y a las 11. La excursión dura cinco horas.
2:00 P.M. Para los que permanecen en **EL PARADOR** la comida se sirve en el restaurante "Rincón Norteño".
4:00 P.M. Inicio del torneo de natación. Piscina.
6:00 P.M. Noche de campamento. Asegúrense temprano de poner su nombre en la lista. Sólo hay cupo para veinte personas. Cabalgaremos hasta la cima de la montaña Colmillo de Cascabel. Será una noche inolvidable entre leyendas, cuentos, juegos y alguno que otro chiste.
7:00 P.M. Cena en el salón Rarámuri.
9:00 P.M. Improvisaremos una obra de teatro. Si tienen inclinaciones artísticas, ésta es la noche ideal para explorarlas. Anfiteatro al aire libre.

Domingo 30 de junio

7:00 A.M. Desayuno. Salón Basaseachic.
8:00 A.M. Torneo de tenis. Finales.
9:00 A.M. Excursión a las Cuevas de Mapimí. Para todos los que no asistieron durante el sábado.
10:00 A.M. Tiempo libre para los que permanecen en **EL PARADOR**.

REALIA

Realia 5-3

Alertan por amenaza de mal tiempo

Minerva Patroni / Diario de Balovento.

De acuerdo al pronóstico del tiempo, para hoy y mañana se esperan los últimos efectos del huracán Douglas en la región. El departamento de Protección Civil está en estado de alerta para activar el plan de emergencia.

Existe un 30 por ciento de probabilidades de recibir una fuerte tormenta en la zona de Balovento dijo el meteorólogo de la universidad local, Gibrán Magullón.

Inundaciones en Costa del Mono. Allí más de mil familias quedaron sin casa ayer.

Cerca de mil familias están en peligro de perder sus casas por inundaciones o derrumbes de cerros, dijo la subdirectora de Protección Civil, Lourdes Sabine Mora.

De continuar la lluvia en Balovento habrá que efectuar evacuaciones, dijo Sabine Mora. Dijo también, que hay tres iglesias y un colegio preparados para refugiar a las personas afectadas por el mal tiempo.

Sabine Mora dijo además que los refugios están preparados con comida, cobijas y ropa.

En general, recomendó no salir de sus casas, el mal tiempo de lluvias no va a pasar pronto. El índice de lluvia marca que estamos sobre el récord de septiembre del año pasado.

El servicio meteorológico dijo que durante el mal tiempo se van a presentar tormentas eléctricas.

Para hoy la temperatura máxima será entre 28 y 32 grados centígrados y la mínima de 23 a 25 grados. Se pronostica buen tiempo para el mes próximo.

Realia 5-1: El Aventurero

1. **Speaking:** Have students look over the cartoon and tell you where they think **El Aventurero** is going and what are the things he likes to do.

2. **Reading/Group work:** Divide the class into groups of three or four students and assign a caption in the realia to each team member. Ask each student to read his or her caption, paying special attention to new vocabulary. Based on their captions have each student explain to the rest of the team what they think **El Aventurero** likes to do and how often he does it.

3. **Writing/Group work:** Have each student write a list of the things he or she likes to do with friends. Have students share the list with the rest of the team and compare answers. Have teams write two or three new captions for **El Aventurero** and present them to the rest of the class.

4. **Listening:** Using the realia ask students how often they do the things **El Aventurero** does. For example: **El Aventurero siempre come comida nutritiva. ¿Tú, con qué frecuencia comes comida nutritiva?**

Realia 5-2: El Parador

1. **Reading:** Ask students if they recognize what kind of place **El Parador** is and what some of the activities are that they can do there. As they identify known vocabulary and cognates, write their answers on the board. Ask students if they think **El Parador** sounds like a fun place.

2. **Listening:** Describe an activity on the calendar of events and have students give the day and time of the event.

3. **Listening/Speaking:** Give students a particular day and time and ask them what they can do then. They should mention the date, time and activity.

4. **Pair work/Speaking/Writing:** Have pairs of students pretend they are students at the school visiting **El Parador** and make plans for the day. Have them plan their morning or their afternoon and write a schedule that tells where they will be at any particular time.

Using Realia 5-3

Realia 5-3: Newspaper article

1. **Reading:** Have students read over the article and underline new vocabulary. Ask students to make a list of the new words and share it with the class. Make a new vocabulary list on the board and have students add the words that are not included in their own list.

2. **Listening/Speaking:** Check for comprehension by asking questions about the article. What is it about? Where is the hurricane happening? What are the dangers faced by the community? Ask students if they have been in a situation such as the one described in the newspaper.

3. **Culture:** Based on the Culture Notes in the textbook, ask students to identify the continent where Balovento is. Challenge them to identify the country.

4. **Writing:** Have students write a report on the weather conditions in their hometown for a particular day, month or season.

REALIA

MUNDO JOVEN...

MATI, NUESTRA LECTORA DEL MES HABLA DE SU FAMILIA: "SOMOS SUPER DIFERENTES PERO MUY UNIDOS..."

MATI HALL, UNA LECTORA DE TAMPA, ES LA GANADORA DEL CONCURSO "LA FAMILIA MÁS ORIGINAL". DI TÚ SI NO TENEMOS RAZÓN:

• •

"Tengo un hermano que quiero mucho, Jonathan. Jonathan es dos meses mayor que yo... ¿qué raro verdad? Bueno, es que los dos somos adoptados. Mis padres, Mark y Guadalupe Hall, — mi mamá es mexicana — decidieron adoptar en lugar de tener hijos propios. A mi papá le gusta que la gente le pregunte por qué todos somos tan diferentes. Siempre tiene una respuesta original porque es muy gracioso. Cuando salimos a restaurantes o a lugares públicos la gente siempre nos mira, imagínense, yo soy asiática, Jonathan afro-americano, mi mamá de México y mi padre norteamericano de pelo rubio. ¡Somos una ensalada! Bueno, les mando una foto mía y de Jonathan, ojalá que ganemos el concurso, tengo muchas ganas de conocer México y practicar mi español. Lo escribo bien ¿no?

• •

¡LO ESCRIBES EXCEPCIONAL, MATI! Y CLARO, TÚ Y TU FAMILA ESTARÁN MUY PRONTO VISITÁNDONOS EN EL D.F. ¡CHAO!

REALIA

Realia 6-2

Cómo brillan nuestros deportistas hispanos

Pablo Morales

Mary Joe Fernández

Alto, delgado y de gran fuerza espiritual, lo más impresionante de este atleta hispano es su capacidad para salir de los momentos difíciles. En los Juegos Olímpicos de 1992 Pablo dedicó su medalla de oro a la memoria de su madre, Blanca, quien murió de cáncer. Aunque ella no estaba allí, Pablo sabía que ella estaba contenta. Hoy, el gran nadador es un empresario de éxito en la industria de los productos acuáticos.

Esta deportista, hija de madre cubana y padre español, ha ganado dos medallas de oro consecutivas en dobles de tenis en las Olimpiadas de 1992 y 1996. Mary Joe es considerada una de las mejores tenistas de hoy. Aunque es delgada tiene brazos fuertes. Es joven y ha ganado torneos en todo el mundo.

LIMPIEZA DE CASA

Profesional con 15 años de experiencia ofrece servicios de limpieza de casa y aseos generales- alfombras, tapiz, cortinas, muebles de todas las piezas. Puede transformar su hogar y hacer más cómodo el estar en casa.

¡Empiece ahora!

También ofrece servicios de jardín
Teléfono 3342304. Los Condes

Using Realia 6-1, 6-2

Realia 6-1: Mundo Joven

1. **Listening:** Before distributing the article to students, draw a two-generation family tree with blank boxes for parents and two siblings on the board. Ask students to copy the drawing in their notebooks. Read the article to the class and ask them to fill in the boxes as they identify the names of the family members. Also, ask them to fill in as much information as they can about each one of the family members.

2. **Reading:** Distribute a copy of the article and have students self-check the information they gathered in the previous listening activity. Remind them to look for cognates and known vocabulary. Ask them to identify, if possible, one more characteristic that describes the family. Ask them what makes the family in the article so unique.

3. **Writing:** Explain to students that the family in the article won a trip to Mexico City. Ask them to write a letter describing their own family (or an imaginary family) to the magazine **Mundo Joven**. Remind them that they have to focus their letter on what makes their family unique.

4. **Speaking/Group work:** Divide the class into groups of three or four. Have students share their letters with the group members and vote on which is the most original family in their group. Ask the winner of each group to describe their family to the class.

Realia 6-2: Hispanic athletes

1. **Listening:** Read the article aloud. Ask students to take notes on what they hear you say about Pablo Morales and Mary Joe Fernández. Tell them to list cognates. Check to see what cognates they heard correctly and write them on the blackboard. Ask what facts they know about Mary Joe and Pablo.

2. **Reading:** Have the class read the article, noticing cognates they did not recognize before. Explain important unfamiliar words, for example, **brillan; industria, acuáticos, medallas**. Using vocabulary studied, ask questions to check their comprehension. **¿Qué deporte practica Mary Joe? ¿Quién sirve de inspiración a Pablo? ¿Por qué? Etc.**

3. **Writing:** Ask each student to write a composition about his/her favorite athlete. Tell the class to use vocabulary studied as well as words and phrases they have learned in the reading. Ask one or more students to report on what they wrote, without giving the name of their favorite athlete. Have the class guess the athlete's name and ask if others wrote about him or her. Ask what additional information they included in their compositions.

Realia 6-3: Housecleaning service ad

1. **Listening:** Before distributing copies to students, read the ad aloud to see if they can guess the topic of the ad.

2. **Listening/Reading:** Call out a specific household chore and ask the students if this ad offers that service.

3. **Speaking:** Have students name all the housecleaning services that this ad offers.

4. **Writing:** Have students write their own announcement advertising their own housecleaning service or some other household service.

REALIA

Situation Cards

Situation Cards 1-1, 1-2, 1-3: Interview

Situation 1-1: Interview

I am a new student at your school. I want to make new friends, so I talk to you, trying to break the ice. How do you respond to my questions?

Buenas tardes.
¿Cómo estás?
Soy... ¿Cómo te llamas tú?
(Introduce me to someone else in the class.)
Bueno, tengo que irme. Hasta luego.

Situation 1-2: Interview

I want to get to know you and your friends a little better, so I'm asking you some questions. How do you respond?

Yo tengo ... años. ¿Y tú? ¿Cuántos años tienes?
Yo soy de... ¿De dónde eres?
¿Cómo se llama tu amigo(a)?
¿Cuántos años tiene...?
¿De dónde es...?

Situation 1-3: Interview

I want to find out what you like and don't like. How do you respond to these questions?

¿Qué te gusta?
¿Te gusta la comida italiana?
¿Qué no te gusta?
¿Te gusta el baloncesto?
¿Te gusta la clase de inglés?

SITUATION CARDS

Situation Cards 1-1, 1-2, 1-3: Role-playing

Situation 1-1: Role-playing

Student A You're at a party one afternoon and someone introduces you to **Student B**. You greet **Student B** and ask how he or she is doing. Then ask what his or her name is. Respond to the questions that **Student B** asks you. Then respond appropriately to the last thing that **Student B** says to you.

Student B You're at a party one afternoon and you get introduced to **Student A**. Answer his or her questions, then find out **Student A's** name. When **Student A** answers, say that you're pleased to meet him or her.

- -

Situation 1-2: Role-playing

Student A **Student B** sits down next to you in the school cafeteria. You haven't met yet, but you know that **Student B** is in your English class. Greet **Student B** and tell him or her your name. Ask **Student B** his or her name and find out how old he or she is.

Student B You're a new student at school. In the cafeteria you sit next to **Student A**, a student from your English class whom you haven't met yet. Answer **Student A's** questions and then find out how old he or she is.

- -

Situation 1-3: Role-playing

Student A You and **Student B** want to go out to eat. Find out if he or she likes the following kinds of food: Italian, Chinese, Mexican. After hearing **Student B's** responses, tell him or her that you also like pizza.

Student B You and **Student A** want to go out to eat. Your friend asks you several questions about what kind of food you like. Answer the questions and then tell **Student A** that you like pizza very much. Ask **Student A** if he or she likes pizza too.

S I T U A T I O N   C A R D S

Situation Cards 2-1, 2-2, 2-3: Interview

Situation 2-1: Interview

You and I are going to go shopping for school supplies together. I want to know what things you need and what you already have. How would you answer my questions?

¿Tienes bolígrafos y papel para la clase de inglés?
¿Cuántos cuadernos necesitas para el colegio?
¿Qué necesitas para la clase de español?
¿Quieres una mochila nueva?

Situation 2-2: Interview

I want to know what your room at home is like, and I want you to tell me a little about your school. You can create an imaginary room or school if you wish. Respond to my questions.

¿Qué hay en tu cuarto?
¿Cuántos carteles hay en la clase de español?
¿Tienes mucha tarea en la clase de inglés?

Situation 2-3: Interview

I want to know what you want and need to do today.

¿Qué quieres hacer?
¿Qué necesitas hacer primero?
¿Necesitas organizar tu cuarto?

Situation Cards 2-1, 2-2, 2-3: Role-playing

Situation 2-1: Role-playing

Student A Imagine it is the first day of school and you and **Student B** are discussing what school supplies you have and don't have. Greet **Student B** and then ask her or him what supplies she or he has for school. Then answer the question **Student B** asks you.

Student B Imagine it is the first day of school and you and **Student A** are discussing what school supplies you have and don't have. After greeting **Student A**, answer her or his question with at least four items. Then ask **Student A** what school supplies she or he doesn't have.

Situation 2-2: Role-playing

Student A You and **Student B** are comparing your rooms. By asking questions, find out if **Student B** has a TV, a table, some posters, a clock, or a desk in his or her room.

Student B You and **Student A** are comparing your rooms. First, answer his or her questions, then ask **Student A** if he or she has a lamp, a radio, or some magazines in the room.

Situation 2-3: Role-playing

Student A You are discussing what you want to do after school with **Student B**. Tell him or her what you need to do first, then at least two things you want to do. Then ask **Student B** what he or she needs and wants to do after school today.

Student B You and **Student A** are discussing what you need and want to do after school. Listen to **Student A's** plans and then answer her or his question with at least two things you need to do and two things that you want to do.

SITUATION CARDS

Situation Cards 3-1, 3-2, 3-3: Interviews

Situation 3-1: Interview

It's the morning of the first day of school and I'm talking to you in the hallway just as the bell is about to ring. I want to find out what this semester will be like for you. Respond to my questions.

¿Qué clases tienes este semestre?
Y hoy, ¿qué clase tienes primero?
Y después, ¿qué clases tienes?
¿Qué hora es?

Situation 3-2: Interview

As we are walking from one class to another, I ask you questions about your schedule for this semester. Answer my questions.

¿A qué hora tienes...?
¿Qué clase tienes a la una?
¿A qué hora tienes el almuerzo?
¿Tienes prisa?

Situation 3-3: Interview

It's now the end of the first week of classes. I'm trying to get to know you better, so I ask you questions about yourself and about your impressions of the school: classes, teachers, classmates.

¿Cómo es la clase de ...?
¿Cómo son los profesores este semestre?
¿Cuál es tu clase favorita? ¿Por qué?
¿Te gustan los deportes/las fiestas/los conciertos/las novelas?

Situation Cards 3-1, 3-2, 3-3: Role-playing

Situation 3-1: Role-playing

Student A You and **Student B** meet and compare your school schedules. Greet each other. Then answer his or her question. Ask what classes he or she has this semester. Listen to your friend's reply and then answer his or her question about the time.

Student B You run into **Student A** and compare school schedules. After answering your friend's greeting, ask him or her what classes he or she has this semester. Tell your friend what classes you have this semester, then ask him or her what time it is. After he or she tells you, say that you have to go.

Situation 3-2: Role-playing

Student A You and **Student B** are trying to complete a school schedule together. Your friend knows what the classes are, and you know when the classes meet. Answer your partner's questions, using the following times:
1. 10:00 A.M. 2. 1:30 P.M. 3. 8:45 A.M. 4. 3:10 P.M.

Student B You and **Student A** are trying to complete a school schedule. You know what the classes are and your partner knows at what time the classes meet. Ask your partner at what time the following classes are:
1. Spanish 2. Math 3. Computer Science 4. Art

Situation 3-3: Role-playing

Student A You and **Student B** are discussing your teachers. Begin the conversation by asking your partner what your Spanish teacher is like. Then answer your partner's question with at least three descriptive adjectives.

Student B You and **Student A** are discussing your teachers. Tell your partner at least three qualities that your Spanish teacher has. Then ask your partner what his or her English teacher is like.

SITUATION CARDS

Situation Cards 4-1, 4-2, 4-3: Interviews

Situation 4-1: Interview

I am an exhange student interested in finding out what a typical teenager from the United States does outside of class. How would you answer these questions?

¿Qué te gusta hacer con tus amigos?
¿Te gusta mirar la televisión en tu tiempo libre?
¿Tocas el piano?
¿Qué deportes practicas?

Situation 4-2: Interview

I need your help in locating some things. Tell me where they are.

¿Hay una piscina cerca de tu casa?
¿Tu casa está lejos o cerca de la escuela?
¿Qué hay encima de tu escritorio?
¿Dónde está tu libro de español?
¿Quién está al lado de...? (*name a student in the class*)

Situation 4-3: Interview

Tell me where and when you do the following activities at the mentioned times.

¿Cuándo vas al cine?
¿Cuándo practicas los deportes?
¿Dónde estás los lunes a las diez de la mañana?
¿Qué haces los sábados por la noche?

Situation Cards 4-1, 4-2, 4-3: Role-playing ◆

Situation 4-1: Role-playing

Student A   You and **Student B** are discussing what each of you does in your free time. Ask **Student B** what he or she does.

Student B   You respond to **Student A** and say what you do in your free time. Then ask **Student A** what he or she does.

¿Que haces...?   descanso   hablo por teléfono
¿Qué te gusta hacer?   camino con el perro   trabajo

Situation 4-2: Role-playing

Student A   You are new in town and want to find out where some places are located. Ask **Student B** if the following places are far from or close to the school: the movie theater, the swimming pool, the post office.

Student B   Listen to **Student A**'s questions and tell him or her if the places are far from or close to the school.

cerca de   lejos de

Situation 4-3: Role-playing

Student A   You and **Student B** are discussing plans for the weekend. Ask **Student B** where he or she is going Saturday night.

Student B   Answer **Student A**'s questions and then ask where he or she is going on Sunday.

¿Adónde vas?

SITUATION CARDS

Situation Cards 5-1, 5-2, 5-3: Interview

Situation 5-1: Interview

I am conducting a survey in order to know more about you and your classmates. I would like to know what things you do and how frequently you do them. Help me by answering the following questions.

¿Quiénes en la clase tocan la guitarra?

¿Quién cuida a su hermano/a durante la semana?

¿Ayudas en casa todos los días?

¿Con qué frecuencia hablas por teléfono?

Situation 5-2: Interview

I am a foreign visitor and I am curious about what you and your friends like to do together. How would you answer these questions?

¿Qué les gusta hacer durante el fin de semana?

¿Les gusta hacer ejercicio juntos?

¿Escriben cartas o miran la televisión los sábados por la noche?

¿Siempre leen las tiras cómicas los domingos?

Situation 5-3: Interview

My family is thinking about moving to your city. Can you give me some information about the weather?

¿Qué tiempo hace en la primavera?

¿Nieva mucho en el invierno?

¿Hace buen tiempo en el verano?

¿En qué meses hace calor?

SITUATION CARDS

Situation Cards 5-1, 5-2, 5-3: Role-playing

Situation 5-1: Role-playing

Student A   You and **Student B** want to compare how often you do certain activities. Choose three of the following activities and ask **Student B** how often he or she does them: ride a bike, study in the library, organize your room, spend time with friends, take the bus to school.

Student B   You and **Student A** want to compare how often you do certain activities. Answer **Student A**'s questions and then find out how often he or she does three of the activities.

¿Con qué frecuencia?   nunca   siempre   a veces

Situation 5-2: Role-playing

Student A   Interview **Student B** and find out which of the following he or she likes to do: to read newspapers or magazines, to exercise or to scuba dive, to read the comics or to write postcards. Then answer **Student B**'s questions.

Student B   Answer **Student A**'s questions, telling which you prefer. Then ask which of the following **Student B** likes: to fish or to ski, to run along the beach or to run in the park, to study or to do aerobic exercises.

¿Te gusta más...?   pescar   bucear   leer revistas
leer las tiras cómicas

Situation 5-3: Role-playing

Student A   Pretend you are traveling to the United States for the very first time. You want to know what the weather is like in several cities during the spring and summer so you can decide which ones to visit. Ask **Student B** about the weather in the following places: Miami, Alaska, Chicago, San Antonio.

Student B   **Student A** is traveling to the United States for the first time. Answer his or her questions about the weather in the spring and summer. Then switch roles.

¿Qué tiempo hace...?   Llueve.   Nieva.
Hace fresco.   Hace mucho viento.   Hace calor.

SITUATION CARDS

Situation Cards 6-1, 6-2, 6-3: Role-playing

Situation 6-1: Role-playing

Student A   You and **Student B** are talking about your families, real or imaginary. Ask **Student B** if he or she has a large or small family. Also find out how many brothers and/or sisters **Student B** has. Ask if he or she has a cat or dog. Then answer **Student B**'s questions.

Student B   You and **Student A** are talking about your real or imaginary families. Answer **Student A**'s questions about your family and then ask him or her how many people are in his or her family. Also ask how old his or her brothers and/or sisters are.

¿Tienes...?   ¿Cuántos/as?

Situation 6-2: Role-playing

Student A   Imagine you are talking long distance to **Student B** who is an exchange student coming to live with you soon. Introduce yourself and give **Student B** a detailed description of yourself and your personality. Then ask **Student B** what he or she is like.

Student B   Imagine you are an exchange student talking long distance to **Student A** who soon will be your host in the U.S. Listen to his or her description and then answer **Student A**'s question.

Tengo...   los ojos   travieso/a   cariñoso/a

Situation 6-3: Role-playing

Student A   You and **Student B** are comparing the things you have to do around the house to help out. Tell **Student B** two chores that you do and then ask **Student B** what he or she does.

Student B   You and **Student A** are comparing chores you do around the house. Listen to what **Student A** does and then answer his or her question, telling two or three things you do to help out.

lavar   limpiar   pasar la aspiradora

SITUATION CARDS

Situation Cards 6-1, 6-2, 6-3: Interview

Situation 6-1: Interview

Tell me about your family or an imaginary one.

¿Cuántas personas hay en tu familia?
¿Quiénes son?
¿Tienen ustedes un perro o un gato?
¿Quién en tu familia es cómico?

Situation 6-2: Interview

Think of a person you know well and really like and answer my questions about that person.

¿Cómo se llama tu amigo/a?
¿Cuántos años tiene?
¿De qué color son los ojos?
¿Cómo es? Por ejemplo, ¿es travieso o cómico?

Situation 6-3: Interview

I need your advice. Tell me what I should do in each situation.

Tengo un examen mañana en la clase de biología, pero quiero salir con mis amigos. ¿Qué debo hacer?
Mis abuelos van a visitar esta noche, pero la casa es un desastre. ¿Qué debemos hacer?
Quiero ir al centro comercial con mi amigo, pero tengo mucha tarea. ¿Qué debo hacer?

S I T U A T I O N   C A R D S